Shamanic Oracle

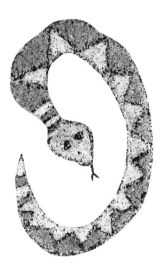

Wulfing von Rohr

Shamanic Oracle

Red Indian Soul Images
from Santa Fe

Illustrations by
Kenneth Joseph Estrada

www.tarotworld.com

First edition

ISBN 3-905219-86-7 / art. no 30.407

© 1999 Urania Verlags AG, Neuhausen am Rheinfall / Switzerland

Original in German, first edition published by
Urania Verlags AG, Neuhausen am Rheinfall / Switzerland

© 2001 for the English version, published by
AGM AGMüller
CH-8212 Neuhausen am Rheinfall / Switzerland
www.tarotworld.com

Printed in Italy

Contents

The Land of Enchantment – Acknowledgements

How can you buy or sell the sky, the warmth of the land? [...] The idea is strange to us. If we do not own the freshness of the air and the sparkle of the water, how can you buy them from us? [...] Every part of this earth is sacred to my people...

[...] This we know. The earth does not belong to the white man, the white man belongs to the earth. All things are connected like the blood which unites our family. [...] Man did not weave the web of life; he is merely a strand in it. Whatever he does to the web, he does to himself.

Excerpt from a letter by Chief Seattle to the US President

Twelve wonderful, exciting years in Santa Fe, New Mexico, being enchanted in the *Land of Enchantment*, have quite decisively shaped an important phase of my life. These twelve years have helped me gain a deep understanding of the great variety of human relations, of the unity of mankind, of all life on earth, and even of the creative unity of all being way beyond this blue planet, reaching far into the dark cosmos, into the night sky with its mysteriously sparkling stars.

I feel immensely grateful for this: grateful to the people, to the land, to the earth, to the sky, the moon, the sun and the stars, to the good spirits, to the Great Spirit...

Here, where the sky is high, wide and transparent blue, where the sun is glaring and the storms are fierce, where the landscape has remained untouched and the air is clear, where life has still preserved its magic... here, where for thousands of years the Rio Grande has carved its path through deep canyons all the way to the Gulf of Mexico, where you come across Red Indian Kivas and

Spanish churches, Buddhist temples and Jewish synagogues, Indian meditation halls and Islamic mosques, where you meet Red Indians and Americans, Asians and Europeans, where you can learn from shamans and priests, from rabbis and gurus, healers and astrologers...here, there is a very special vibration, a very unusual place of power!

Chief Seattle's words are particularly significant in Santa Fe. Here, they not only refer to the outer land and to the community of people, which deserve to be appreciated and cared for, but to the inner land of the soul which waits to be cared for and experienced with amazement. His words are a warning to us not to sell our soul, but to open up to its wonders.

While shooting a year-long Terra-X broadcast for the ZDF (a major German TV channel) on the mysterious Anasazi-Indians of the Chaco Canyon, whose traces had been lost since the 13th century, I had the opportunity to explore numerous ancient settlement areas and places of worship. I came in touch with many informed people, among them anthropologists of the Red Indians. As a result I received additional hints about the paths of the shamans that go beyond specific rituals and ceremonies.

In all cultures and traditions shamans are those men and women who have opened up to the mystery of the spirit in the body, to the sky in the earth, who have walked over invisible bridges from this side of life to the other side, who, by passing nebulous spaces between life and death, have found another reality.

The shamans, the "magicians" and "masters" of all spiritual paths, have explored these mysteries and made them available to other people. The Shamanic Oracle at hand came to life from the experiences of these twelve years in Santa Fe. Its illustrations are mainly taken from Red Indian archetypes. But its wisdom goes way beyond them.

The path of the shaman stands for a spiritual attitude, an openness to everything, to life as a whole. On this path primeval images, archetypes, symbols and signs serve as milestones, as signposts in the labyrinths of the mists of moods and feelings.

The outer circumstances of our lives, our individual tasks and challenges, our joys and sorrows might differ from one person to another. But with regard to our inner processes, to the development of the soul, with regard to our hopes and dreams, our aims and ideals we are all the same. We all want to be happy. As a part of this, we want to find meaning and fulfillment even beyond the great transformation of physical death.

The Shamanic Oracle is offering us its help in this by bringing to life images of our soul lying deep within us. It helps us in our very personal vision quest, our spiritual search by activating powers that we already have inside us, by awakening our intuition and giving us new inspiration.

I would like to take this opportunity to express my deepest gratitude to some people from Santa Fe who have helped me in a very special way to continue walking the path of the shaman. Their contribution to the birth of this shamanic oracle was mostly indirect, and yet clearly noticeable to me:

Chris and Karin Griscom, whose first foreign client at the Light Institute of Galisteo in February 1986 was me; the oriental carpet dealer and spiritual seeker Sharon Z. Schenk and her daughters Zahira and Maryam; Martín Prechtel, a shaman, artist and musician, I had mentioned in the ZDF broadcast and since then has been coming to Europe from time to time; Gayan Sylvie Winter, a lively and committed wanderer between worlds who co-designed the *Tarot of Love* and the *Power of Angels – cards* with me; Chaitanya H. Deuter, a wonderful musician, whose CD *Land of Enchantment* captures Santa Fe in all its magic; Ann Aura Knight with her sons Marco and Brian, who is carrying the wonderful legacy of being a Red Indian Princess and whose work will – hopefully – lead her back to Europe soon; Alan Oken, an exceptionally knowledgeable, intuitive and humorous astrologer and "New World Server" and the exceptionally gifted artist, Kenneth Joseph Estrada. *Ken, thanks for the Buffalo!*

My acknowledgements would be incomplete, though, if I did not name two people who have been sharing with me their light and love, their inspiration and transformation since the Eighties: Sant Darshan Singh and Sant Rajinder Singh. They are shamans in the highest sense: They live and teach "positive mysticism". This means that they have both feet firmly on the ground and share their love from their hearts with every being: with all human beings, all animals, all plants. They serve them all selflessly and – at the same time – are one with Father Sky and the Great Spirit in the consciousness of their soul, in their spirit. They safely guide the spirit of the seeker through the perils of the in between worlds, of the dreamworlds and the worlds beyond, until it, too, has become one with the Great Spirit.

Last but not least: *Thank you, Santa Fe!*

Mother Earth, Father Sky

Earth teach me quiet, as the grasses are still with new light.
Earth teach me suffering, as old stones suffer with memory.
Earth teach me humility, as blossoms are humble with beginning.
Earth teach me caring, as mothers nurture their young.
Earth teach me courage, as the tree which stands alone.
Earth teach me limitation, as the ant which crawls on the ground.
Earth teach me freedom, as the eagle which soars in the sky.
Earth teach me acceptance, as the leaves which die in the fall.
Earth teach me renewal, as the seed which rises in the spring.
Earth teach me to forget myself, as melted snow forgets its life.
Earth teach me to remember kindness, as dry fields weep with rain.

Prayer of Ute

I arise from rest with movements
Swift as the beat of raven wings.
I arise to meet the day,
Houa. Houa.
My face is turned from the dark of night
To gaze at the dawn of day
Now lightening the sky.

Song of the Inuit
(from: Shared Spirits, Wildlife and Native Americans, pg. 5, pg. 6,
Dennis L. Olson, North Word Press, Minocqua, Wisconsin, 1995)

Between earth and sky, sky and earth, our life goes on and on, never standing still. Every day brings us wonderful and significant experiences on many levels: the material, the emotional, the mental and the spiritual. We are moving in earthly and heavenly realms, passing through them – however, often without being aware of it.

As the elders have been telling us insistently, each one of us is playing a small, yet important and necessary part in a huge world-theater of light and shadow. Sometimes we might perceive it as a tragedy, sometimes as a comedy and many times as both. We are actors on this grand stage of life. And sooner or later – unfortunately for most of us, being mentally lethargic, it will be later – we will discover that we are an intrinsic part of a single all-embracing breathtaking creative force. We might call this force God or Allah, Jahweh or Buddha-power. The name Great Spirit is equally appropriate.

If we are supposed to be a drop from the sea of eternity, a ray of light from an eternally shining sun, why then are we so full of fears on our journey through life? Why then are we sometimes so full of rage, so confused or even depressed? If "in reality" we are part of a wonderful creative force, why then do we perceive ourselves so many times as "victims" of outer circumstances or "accidental" strokes of fate?

Because we have lost touch with values and visions; because we have forgotten our dreams and goals; because we got lost and do not walk on our path; because we do not know the meaning of the path any more.

We keep avoiding the challenge of becoming ourselves totally, because we are too busy with merely surviving, or groaning under the burden of our daily life.

Or simply, because we have more or less become the driftwood of a society that has made consumption and comfort, short-term satisfaction of the senses and superficial materialism an end in itself.

Wise women and men, prophets and seers of ancient and modern times have found ways and means to overcome physical and mental inertia. They have developed exercises and methods in order to attain emotional and mental clarity and to gain a new spiritual orientation. *Sweatlodges* are part of this development; so is the *Vision Quest* – a conscious, though initially even aimless (as it is entirely open!) search for spiritual meaning and a new life force, which eventually, if successful, may even become a personal medicine.

The search for a spiritual vision of life, the active endeavor to find a hidden source of spiritual revival, the demand for clear progress, the longing to become again one with the Great Spirit and to let it live through us – all this describes the *Path of the Shaman*.

This hidden source of conscious life in harmony with Father Sky and Mother Earth can be called *The Holy Grail, The Philosopher's Stone, The Jewel in the Lotus Flower* or *The Power of the Medicine Wheel*.

The process of the search may take different shapes. The longing of the soul may express itself in the process of *creative visualization* or in *active imagination*, in dreams and their interpretation or in prayer, in the selfless service to fellow human beings or in silent meditation.

Images will always be involved – outer and inner ones. The soul abides in a complex world of colored images and powerful symbols. Old shamanic rituals as well as Jungian psychology make use of certain signs and archetypes that can help us overcome our spiritual inertia. They can direct our attention back to the true way and encourage us to give back to our life its true meaning.

The Path of the Shaman neither allows a cheap escape from our tasks, nor will it somehow magically support us in solving our problems or fulfill our wishes or make our dreams come true with no effort from our side.

On the contrary, the Path of the Shaman challenges us to take again responsibility for ourselves, for our thoughts, words and actions, for our entire life journey and for all decisions we make.

If we want to reach for the stars – and we ought to do that; we are allowed to and we are capable of doing so! – then, accordingly, we have to work hard for it, we have to put something of ourselves aside, we need dedication and patience. Mainly, the Path of the Shaman is calling on us to live more consciously, more sensitively and carefully and to open up to the creative forces of the Great Spirit.

The Shamanic Oracle can be a valuable support in this respect as it points out hidden gifts of the seeker or questioner that have never been discovered before or that have been buried over the years. It shows us the challenges we have refused to take in the past, our incomplete tasks and the lost visions of our soul, as well as our chances for development. The Shamanic Oracle is a kind of magnifying glass to detect the strong and the weak sides of our personality. At the same time it functions like spiritual binoculars making the normally still vaguely discernible path and the far away goal visible and thus tangible. The Shamanic Oracle takes a look at important issues, essential qualities and true goals in our life; it provides us with the tools to find meaning and to make this meaning come true.

Its profound symbols and complex images trigger the recognition of realities the soul had long ago forgotten. Its impressive figures, earthy colors, vivid structures and strong sensual powers activate unconscious and superconscious realities that can again become a natural part of our life-journey, the goal of all life: self-awareness and self-realization, selflessly serving Mother Earth and Father Sky and all beings alive and, finally, disappearing into the Great Spirit.

Now, how can we benefit from the shamans' magic in our modern world? Going into the forty pictures of the Shamanic Oracle can effectively help us to rediscover powers buried within ourselves. They serve as an impetus for taking a new vision; they encourage us to develop a new sense for what is essential. In the context of an appropriate question the cards help us to find answers, develop a new dynamic in our life and to go our very own way. The pictures of the Shamanic Oracle then even serve as a personal medicine!

Martin Buber, an outstanding representative of Jewish mysticism, describes the value of the individual search for truth as follows:

"God does not say, 'You can reach me this way, but not that way'. He says, 'Everything you do can be a way to reach me, if you do it in a way that leads you to me.'"

The Shamanic Oracle intends to be a useful means for sincere seekers, courageously and curiously advancing on their way. It is a tool to perform the personal transformations that are necessary from time to time and to live a more fulfilling life in tune with sky and earth. It can help us to transform everything we do into a way to truth, if we do it in the right way and with the right consciousness.

The Meaning of the Forty Cards:
From Kokopelli to Zia

It is true that many of the old ways have been lost, but just as the rains restore the earth after a drought, so the power of the great mystery will restore the way and give it new life. We ask that this happen not just for the red people, but for all the people, that they all might live. In ignorance and carelessness they have walked on Inamaka, our Mother. They did not understand that they are part of all beings, the four-legged, the winged, Grandfather Rock, the Tree People, and our Star Brothers. Now our Mother and all our relations are crying out. They cry for the help of all people.

Prayer of the Lakota
Quoted from: Shared Spirits - Wildlife and Native Americans, (page 6)
Dennis L. Olson, NorthWord Press, Minocqua, Wisconsin, 1995;
ISBN 1-55971-474-3

On the following pages you will find illustrations of the forty cards, their names, key words concerning their general meaning and hints regarding their meaning in a specific position in a spread: as card of the day; as Father Sky or Mother Earth; as past, present or future; in the medicine wheel as East, South, West or North; as personal medicine.

According to the prayer of the Lakota the interpretations of the Shamanic Oracle should be understood as an appeal. They are calls to become conscious, to remember our own potential, to revive our original vision of life. The interpretations are positive, constructive and aim to building us up and support us. With this the shadow is not denied, but the forces of light are enforced within us and on the earth.

Animal Trails

Animal trails indicate that there is life all around us. Many times these trails are overlooked or taken in the wrong way.

In the Shamanic Oracle this card means: Follow your path; be very alert which way you are turning and stepping. If you follow a teacher, find out and then check which is his spiritual path and if he is really capable of leading you towards the goal you regard to be your highest.

As Card of the Day

Which trail are you following today? Which direction are you taking? What power is driving you to move on? Think about it, then make a decision.

As Mother Earth

What is it that you are (still) denying about your mother? Look at it as the way that was right for her. What have you learned from your mother? Make use of it. Follow in her tracks.

As Father Sky

What is it that you are (still) denying about your father? Look at it as the way that was right for him. What have you learned from your father? Make use of it. Follow in his tracks.

As East

There are many ways leading to the goal. Look to where your sun is rising. Find your goal first, and you are bound to create your own path.

As South

Which way is your heart pulling you? Follow this strong longing, even if it means you are taking the long way around.

As West

Look at the setting sun. What promise awaits you at the glowing horizon?

As North

Look up at the Pole Star. Not all trails point to the front or to the back, left or right; some paths lead you up and in. What is it that leads you there?

As Medicine

Trails appear when you set off on your path; paths develop when you follow the same trail many times. In the course of this month, learn to discern which are the beaten tracks that make you dull and which new paths you can try out in the jungle of life.

Badger

Perseverance and persistence; actually, a soft energy which can become very strong when it is attacked and wants to and has to protect itself and other beings relying on it.

Let us not flag in our search. Let us keep at it and dig deeper, even if we are facing great resistance or are confronted with delays. Only our own intensive endeavor allows us to be open to higher blessings.

As Card of the Day

Make an effort today to be soft, to stay soft and unwavering at the same time without losing sight of your aim.

As Mother Earth

It is totally okay to protect and defend that which you are responsible for. Softness does not mean to be overly compliant or weak.

As Father Sky

Your hands at work, your heart with the people, your spirit in a space beyond the stars – this is the way you should try to live.

As East

"I am not trying to force success, I am simply opening to whatever life wants to give to me on its own accord."

As South

"I am not losing myself in the temporary pleasures of the moment, but gaining more strength through renunciation."

As West

"Telling stories in a circle of friends, I bring back the memories of the wisdom of the elders."

As North

"I write down what moves me and what makes me go on – and ask for the blessings of the Great Spirit."

As Medicine

Which issue in your life is calling you to dig deeper? In the next few days devote yourself mainly to one issue in your life, until you have really solved it.

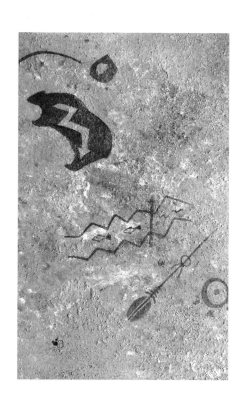

Bear Card

This card points out the existence of a bear specially characterized by a "heart line". The strength of the bear is coming from his heart. When our heart is hurt, our strength fails.

Sustained strength which can protect us throughout our life's journey, arises from the heart. Let us develop compassion for people whose heart has been hurt; let us share with them our strength and ask the Great Spirit to heal them.

As Card of the Day

For one day just follow your heart in everything you think, feel, say and do. Then take stock.

As Mother Earth

You are responsible for weaker beings that you are looking after: no matter if they are adults or children, animals or plants. Take on this task like a mother bear.

As Father Sky

The bear appears in two constellations of the night sky simultaneously: as the Little and as the Great Bear. In this place this card offers you the prospect of healing your soul.

As East

Become absorbed by the picture of a bear. What kind of feelings are coming up, what thoughts, what associations?

As South

Put all your energy into your tasks. You have more energy than you think.

As West

Someone who is hurt and suffers needs your help. Go to him or her.

As North

Learn to withdraw from time to time, from the pompousness and rush of the world into silence, and leave it up to the Great Spirit to give you a sign when it is time for you to turn outwards again.

As Medicine

For four weeks just follow your heart as much as you can in everything you think, feel, say and do. And don't be surprised if people around you start wondering what is going on with you. You will change your life fundamentally.

Blessings of the Earth

For the Pueblo Indians corn is the most sacred fruit on earth. They consider it to be the "bread of life": It serves them as food and can be stored over the winter months; its fibres are used for weaving clothes.

Find out what is the most precious gift Mother Earth has for you. Make sure that you are honoring this gift, that you use it creatively to the fullest and do not throw it away carelessly. What is it that really preserves your life?

As Card of the Day

Bless each bite you take today. Take your time to chew consciously (thirty two times!) feeling grateful for the gifts of the Earth.

As Mother Earth

Invite a female person who is dear to you to a delicious and life-preserving (that is vegetarian) meal. Enjoy the meal as a ritual.

As Father Sky

Invite a man who is dear to you to a healthy and natural (that is vegetarian) meal. Enjoy the meal as a ritual.

As East

As much as possible, today eat only food that has a yellowish color: for example apricots, oranges, pumpkin, ginger, walnuts, quinces, yellow corn, potatoes, yellow lentils.

As South

As much as possible, today eat only food that has a reddish color: peaches, tomatoes, red berries, beetroot, red beans.

As West

As much as possible, today eat only food that is of a black color: black beans, blackberries, blueberries, blackcurrant, cherries and mushrooms, rye bread, blue corn.

As North

As much as possible, eat only white food today: for example milk, curd, cream cheese, kidney beans, coconut, shoots, white radish, cauliflower, white cabbage.

As Medicine

For one month, before each meal (no matter how small it may be) practice stopping for a moment to thank the Earth for its gifts. Observe whether your outlook on life has changed afterwards.

Blossom

A great variety of colors given to us as a gift from Mother Earth. A new stage of life full of joy and lightheartedness.

Let your gifts and talents shine through. Radiate your inner values and your beauty for everyone around to see. Enjoy even the small things in life. For many people the sweetness and the rich colours of the blossoms do not seem to be of much value, and yet we can not only see and smell them, but even taste them. Without them honey would not taste sweet.

As Card of the Day

Try to smile at others the same way a blossom does, making no distinction who it is looking at. In the evening note how your day was.

As Mother Earth

Without bees, flowers bloom only one summer long. We are all part of one great whole, visibly or invisibly depending on each other. Make an active contribution to the great whole.

As Father Sky

From the early sunrise to the late sunset, blossoms follow the course of the sun. Are we following the inner star, the light of the Great Spirit? Are we trying to?

As East

Try to recollect your childhood dreams, cool dewdrops of your hopes for life. Remember them now and let them be a part of your everyday life again.

As South

Try to recollect the feelings, the music and the fragrance of happy moments of laughter and joy. Let these pictures come back to life and build up your strength again.

As West

Collect rose petals and other fragrant blossoms in a bowl. Touch them from time to time, breathe in their tender fragrance and let them be a reminder of life's fullness in hours of contemplation.

As North

Trees stretching out their bare lifeless branches into the winter sky only seem to be dead. They are not; they are simply contemplating their vision and gathering new strength for it. Understand times of withdrawal help you to afterwards continue walking your path with a greater sense of direction.

As Medicine

A blossom is shining and releasing its fragrance not only to make us happy, but also to draw attention to it to make sure its fruit will be received. What is it that you want other people to see, feel and receive from you?

Bridge to the Sky

A bridge to the spiritual world; a rainbow coming from a world beyond, gently touching the physical world we know; a present from our ancestors, an offering of gifts that, although not physically tangible, are a perceptible support for our life.

Our own wisdom will never be enough to touch the sky. For this reason it does make sense to learn from the experience of the elders and to seek the guidance of a shaman who will lead us upwards across the bridge into the sky.

As Card of the Day
Which opportunity, even though it might not be obvious but hidden, is life offering you today to see the deeper meaning?

As Mother Earth
Which woman from history or your family is an example for you? Find out more about her life, her feelings, her visions, her achievements in everyday life, her legacy.

As Father Sky
Which man from history or your family is an example for you? Find out more about his life, his feelings, his visions, his achievements in everyday life, his legacy.

As East
Nourish the power of hope.

As South
Follow the call of love.

As West
Respond to the requirements of duty.

As North

Seek the wisdom of the elders.

As Medicine

Inspiration is a heavenly gift nobody can create or force. It happens when we entrust ourselves to a higher guidance. But first we need to be ready for this. Are you ready to receive guidance?

Buffalo

Security and strength. A gift from the Great Spirit to feed two-legged beings with its body, let them make clothes from his hide and tools from his bones. The herds of buffalo were the basis of survival for the Plains Indians - the tribes of the vast prairies.

Discover all your strengths, use all your material and spiritual resources and do not waste your gifts and skills. Confidence in our strength arises from the insight that the Great Spirit gives us everything we need for living, provided we know how to use it rightly.

As Card of the Day
Start your day by repeating the affirmation "I am" for five minutes. Carry the awareness of "I am" in you. With all you do feel "I am".

As Mother Earth
Be grateful for everything you receive in life. Show this gratitude by sharing with others, not wasting anything.

As Father Sky
Be grateful for everything you receive in life. Show this gratitude by remembering that you alone cannot create anything, that in fact everything is a gift of the Great Spirit.

As East
For a while keep working with the affirmation "I am clarity."

As South
For a while keep working with the affirmation "I am compassion."

As West
For a while keep working with the affirmation "I am service."

As North

For a while keep working with the affirmation "I am peace."

As Medicine

In the medicine wheel the buffalo represents the place of wisdom, continuous renewal and personally gained knowledge.

"Whatever you inherited from your forefathers, make it your own so you can preserve it" goes a saying from Lower Saxony pointing toward the same: Only your own life experience counts, only your own realization – no empty talk.

Centipede

Fast energy that makes many people jump back instinctively; special powers of flexibility. In the figurative sense: a magical ladder or bridge leading down to the "underworld"; death and transformation.

The shadow is challenging you: You need to face the issue of genuine and thorough transformation of the powers of your personality. Discover that which will remain even after your body has decayed.

As Card of the Day

Read the obituaries in today's newspaper: notice how old or young people were who departed from this life; read the aphorisms their relatives wrote for them...

As Mother Earth

Which shadow does the feminine hold for you? Which fears do you associate with the anima, the elemental force of yin? Incorporate this shadow within you, in order to dissolve it.

As East

Meditate on the thought: The rising sun is dissolving my life. This is the last sunrise I will ever see on this earth. How does it make you feel?

As South

For a while contemplate with sincerity: What significance would it have for me to let go of everything I have experienced on this earth? What would change for you?

As West

Let your eyes follow the setting sun. Feel that you, too, are getting ready to go down here one day, just to rise somewhere else again. How does that make you feel?

As North

Imagine yourself lying in a dark grave with your eyes closed yet fully awake in the middle of the night: Do you see the light of the eternal sun in front of your forehead?

As Medicine

For one month live as if it was your last one… How would you act, what would you say, how would you feel…?

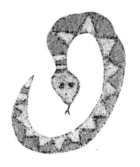

Circle of Unity

A female and a male figure holding hands, symbolizing the union of heart and soul, the unity in the Great Spirit with Father Sky and Mother Earth.

Go and find the person or persons you would like to and are able to join hands with, so that you contribute to the renewal of the original unity of all life.

As Card of the Day

Invite someone you love to a personal meeting: a walk, a visit to the museum, a concert, a cup of tea.

As Mother Earth

Union with women: What is it that unites you with all women? Become aware of at least three things, carry them in your heart for a few days. Observe how your life is changing.

As Father Sky

Union with men: What is it that unites you with all men? Become aware of at least three things, carry them in your heart for a few days. Observe how your life is changing.

As East

Union with the East: What personal points of contact do you have with the East? Which person coming from there would you like to meet, talk to, invite to come here?

As South

Union with the South: With which person coming from the South are you going to make contact soon, to have an exchange? Who will you be able to help by that?

As West

Union with the West: Do you know anyone coming from the West who you would like to know more about or who could tell you something about their home and their life? Start looking for him or her.

As North

Union with the North: Which person or people from the North do you count among your acquaintances or friends? What do you know about life there? Become curious.

As Medicine

Think of the earth we live on, we live off, of the air we breathe that connects us all (after all, we are breathing in the same air someone else was breathing out): Is there any room left for the separation of people? We are all one. Be very conscious about this in the next couple of days.

Dance of Unity

Remembering the original unity that underlies all and everything and that connects everything. Life can be an absolutely lively and cheerful experience: the shaman "dances" with utter lightheartedness from one challenge to the next.

An active endeavor to work together with like-minded people and to make a contribution to our home, the Earth, as a group. Remember to become, to remain and to be cheerful.

As Card of the Day

Do something together in your circle of family or friends that is a harmonious bonding: singing together, a long walk or simply doing something "ordinary".

As Mother Earth

Pay a visit to the local Salvation Army or to another charity-organization and help them for one day to care for people in need: financially, by working in the kitchen or otherwise.

As Father Sky

Go to the hospital or a retirement home and ask if you can help out for one day: doing small jobs or visiting some people, thus bringing light into their day.

As East

Go to mass in an orthodox church. Experience the special liturgy and atmosphere.

As South

Find a mosque in your vicinity and experience the worship of God in an Islamic service.

As West

Take part in a sweatlodge ritual or a ceremony of the medicine wheel, or organize it yourself.

As North

Go to a Tibetan temple and be a witness to the rituals of this form of Buddhism.

As Medicine

In the near future, take part in at least three feasts, dance events, concerts or other events from other cultures other than your own. Open up to the many ways of living joy.

Deer Dance

This ritual dance represents a conscious effort to see oneself as part of a greater unity, where earth, plants, animals and men are dependent on each other for survival.

Tune into the world around you and start sensing its needs. Cultivate traditional rituals or develop new ones of your own to focus your sense again and again on the unity of life.

As Card of the Day

Make a ritual today which has a very personal meaning for you: hug a tree, plant something, light a candle on the altar, pray…

As Mother Earth

A woman in your vicinity wants to send you a message in an indirect way. Look for omens and symbols showing you her message and helping you interpret it.

As Father Sky

A man in your vicinity says or does something with a hidden meaning for you. Use your mind to grasp it.

As East

Be like a reed bending in the wind, yielding and yet not losing touch with its inner strength.

As South

Be like a big tree and give shade to all those beings who have longed for coolness in the heat of the sun at noon. Invite them to take a rest!

As West

Be like a hazelnut tree bearing ripe fruit that nourishes and strengthens men and animals.

As North

Be like the Christmas rose flowering in the middle of a snowy winter, giving light and joy.

As Medicine

Try to overcome your doubts about whether you chose the right way by recalling the visions and inspirations that put you on this path. Find an appropriate ritual to revive their initial powers.

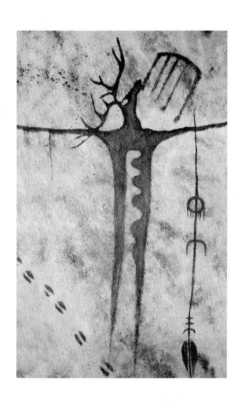

Deer Hunter

A hunter wears a headdress with antlers in order to invoke the spirit of the deer he wants to hunt. He is asking the spirit's permission to let him shoot the deer, thus ensuring the survival of his people.

This card holds two messages for us: Everything we receive comes to us as a gift from the Great Spirit – everything! And there is a great law of resonance: We need to be properly prepared for everything we would like to receive. "Success is what comes on its own accord."

As Card of the Day

Prepare the soil now for a success yet to come. Set off on your path. Even the tiniest step in the right direction will bring you closer to the goal.

As Mother Earth

Help a woman in your vicinity to reach her goal.

As Father Sky

Help a man in your vicinity to reach his goal.

As East

Be patient with your weaknesses: Take your time to work on yourself. And don't expect miracles, but rather a gradual development.

As South

Be humble in view of your fate: Learn to accept events in your life as fate, as something that was sent to you.

As West

Reverence for every living being: Every living being is unique in its own way. Honor and respect that.

As North

Adoration of beauty: Protect the world around you and its treasures, before they are spoiled or wasted.

As Medicine

Stags, deer and antelope teach us patience with our weaknesses, humbleness in view of our fate, reverence for the uniqueness of every living being and adoration for the grace and beauty of nature.

Dragonfly

The neat and trim dragonfly is an indicator of water in our vicinity. If we follow it we will be able to find the water. This makes it a symbol and bearer of good luck.

Look for the signs of life appearing again and again in your everyday life – indications of gifts from Mother Earth and Father Sky that will give you a fresh vitality.

As Card of the Day

Give someone a present: your attention, your affection, your time, your love… Become a bearer of good luck yourself today!

As Mother Earth

The Great Spirit always comes to our aid when we are in trouble or in real need of something. Look out for signs in nature: the flight or call of a bird, a deer or rabbit crossing your path, an exceptional tree.

As Father Sky

Signs do not always take a tangible earthly shape on the outside, but can often come to us in the form of dreams and ideas. In the next few days become aware of unusual ideas and sudden inspirations and try to sense their meaning.

As East

For a while wear only a piece of jewelry or an amulet from India or Bali that you like. What effect does it have on you?

As South

Go and look for a ring or bangle from Africa or Arabia that you find appealing. Watch the effect it has on you.

As West

Chose a brooch or a pendant from the Red Indian part of the American Southwest. How does it make you feel?

As North

Find a piece of jewelry from Ireland, Scotland or the Baltic Sea countries. What do you notice when you are wearing only this one?

As Medicine

The magic of good luck is mainly not to want anything else than what life gives to you. For the next four weeks try to live with this attitude.

Evening Dance

Dance at sunset, thankful for the day and its gifts, thankful for having had the chance of living this day at all!

Complete this day and every one of your days with a prayer of gratitude. Rejoice in the completion of other periods of time and seasons and in return offer your thankfulness to the Great Spirit. Even if you perceive a certain period of time to be somewhat negative, you will gain experiences you can feel grateful for.

As Card of the Day

"Sacrifice" half an hour this evening and take your time to contemplate on the day, to consciously enjoy nature or to meditate in peace.

As Mother Earth

Write down three things that life – people, animals, nature, the Great Spirit – gave you today.

As Father Sky

Write down three things you gave to the world around you today – to people, animals, plants, to the Earth.

As East

What is it that is missing for the next stage of your life? Start looking for it.

As South

Which feelings are a hindrance on your path? Are you ready to let go of them?

As West

Find a new balance between old experience and new enthusiasm.

As North

Write down three goals that are really worth the effort.

As Medicine

Every day, every life on earth comes to an end…
Look out for that which remains. Ask for an insight into this.

Fire

Energy, strength, power. Fire is a herald of the power that transforms the visible into the invisible; it is a flaring up of the Great Light that can either warm or burn, transform or destroy, melt metals or kill people.

In your everyday life and on your spiritual path, learn when and how to use your power energy, but learn how to use it wisely and effectively and without harming anyone or anything. Thoughts and words, feelings and actions can become tremendous powers of fire.

As Card of the Day
Support others all day long, encourage them, but without overwhelming or commanding them.

As Mother Earth
Let yourself be taken by the passion for life. Is it still burning in you? If not, rekindle it. How? By working or serving selflessly, by being in nature, doing sports, dancing or singing.

As Father Sky
Fire melts metal; it transforms wood into light and heat, into embers and ashes. Something is rising up, leaving something else behind. This is the way your thinking and decision making should become.

As East
Do not utter a single word of criticism (however right it may be), without saying something positive about the person, thing or matter.

As South
Go to the sauna or sweatlodge, cleanse yourself outside and inside. Open up for something new.

As West

Let others nourish themselves with the warmth of your heart, help them kindle their joy of life, their courage.

As North

Keep the embers of your inner fire burning overnight under a layer of ashes. Fuel your embers with silent meditation.

As Medicine

Carry out a ritual: Make a fire (preferably in the open air), write down separately all situations and weaknesses that are bothering you; then, one by one, feed the sheets of paper to the fire while saying a prayer of purification. Bury the ashes afterward.

Fisherman

A man with his hands raised in gratitude – for the water, for the food, for success. The fish represents the sustenance which is not always readily available; the spear stands for his effort; the water stands for the cycle of appearing and disappearing, for everything is "in the flow".

Be grateful for whatever life gives to you. Let yourself be taken by the flow of energies that are never standing still. Pursue your goals with full force, and yet be open to the constant changes and the new experiences they will bring to you.

As Card of the Day

Go to a beautiful lake or river and spend some time there. Go inside and feel: What meaning does water have for my life?

As Mother Earth

Do we have permission to kill living beings just because they cannot speak, even though we would survive otherwise? Let us take only that from Mother Earth which is really necessary for our survival.

As Father Sky

The more a person is nourished by the inner source of spiritual strength, the less he /she needs outer nourishment. Find the access to the source that will always refresh and nourish you.

As East

For one or two days live only on water, milk, diluted juices or vegetable broth.

As South

For a while make fruits and nuts your only meal.

As West

For a couple of days eat only vegetables growing above ground.

As North

For a week eat only vegetables growing underground, like roots and potatoes.

As Medicine

The lesson that fish teach man is: What we have together is more than what separates us. In the next few days nourish whatever connects you with people.

Giving Birth

Carrying to term, birthing, birth; playing the role of the mother; protecting, caring, loving. Taking responsibility, giving selfless support to weaker ones needing to be cared for.

Learn to nourish and protect others, to encourage and love them. Think, feel, say and do whatever brings out the best in them.

As Card of the Day

Feel like a mother feels (even if you are a man) toward all living beings you meet. Understand what it means to protect, nourish, give warmth, be there for someone.

As Mother Earth

You are carrying a strength inside that wants to manifest in a very creative way in the social or artistic field. Give it time to slowly take shape before you start carrying it outwards.

As Father Sky

You are carrying a treasure inside that still needs to be discovered. You won't find it in outer action, but rather in inner being.

As East

Cultivate your dreams and visions; guard them so that they can grow into goals and plans.

As South

Once you have started something, don't give up at the first sign of resistance, but keep on putting all you've got into it.

As West

Often it happens that shortly before the completion of a project unexpected problems start surfacing. Now, more than ever, inner persistence and outer letting go are needed for a successful outcome.

As North

If someone disagrees with you, let it be. Don't get entangled in unneccessary discussions, but rather turn your spirit toward its true roots.

As Medicine

There are two kinds of births: the physical and the spiritual. The spiritual one occurs when you start listening to the inner music, seeing the inner light. Find a master shaman who is capable of making this connection for you.

Hand

Symbol for self-expression, action and applied skills; symbol for a child. In the early days of Earth also used as a sign of life indicating the existence of two-legged beings in a certain area.

Do something, be active, make a specific effort to help humanity, take charge of something personally. Make sure that what you do is creative and meaningful. It might also be an indication that a child will come to you.

As Card of the Day
Be aware of everything you take into your hands today: another hand, paper, a pencil, the steering wheel, cutlery…

As Mother Earth
A woman will play a major part in your life, one who knows how to take charge of things, how to get on with them and how to complete them.

As Father Sky
A man will appear in your life who will entrust you with a task or challenge you to accomplish something.

As East
Start the morning with a "prayer to the sun": Stand facing East, lift your head up to the sun and stretch your arms up to the sky with your palms open.

As South
Start your work full of energy. You will succeed in whatever you have intended to accomplish if you do it with all your heart.

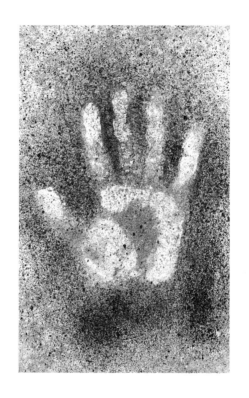

As West

With calmness and serenity safely complete a task you have wanted to complete for a very long time.

As North

At night, before going to bed, kneel down in prayer as the Muslims do: Kneel with your head bent down to the ground and your arms stretched out wide in front of you, your palms touching the earth.

As Medicine

What in your life is really in your hands? How can you improve your actions in the next four weeks, how can you better handle your problems?

Horse

The horse arrived quite late in the Red Indian world of America, but it was quickly integrated not only into everyday life (thus turning agricultural tribes into nomads who hunt buffalo) but also into the shamanic ideology – as a symbol for independence and speed.

Discover your world, making use of all helpers available on your geographical and spiritual travels. But make sure not to misuse your helpers – honor them and take care of them.

As Card of the Day

Escape from your daily grind. For one day shake off the yoke of routine. Feel free today, make yourself free…

As Mother Earth

Move through this earthly life with the agility of a wild horse, tireless and modest and ready to sacrifice all and everything for its freedom.

As Father Sky

Fly through the world of the spirit with the strength of Pegasus, the winged Horse of the Gods. Riding on its back even Mount Olympus won't be too far to reach. Becoming conscious liberates.

As East

First of all make it a point that the "rider" – the spirit – reins and controls the "horse" – body and mind – and not the other way round.

As South

Once you have taken a path, follow its course without stopping constantly and having doubts about it.

As West

Spur your spirit. Don't allow it to succumb to idleness, spur it to move on.

As North

Take your horse to the watering place – let your body and mind take their well deserved rest, thus allowing the spirit to rest, too.

As Medicine

If you are already familiar with horseback-riding, then ride even more in the next weeks – across the open land, far off the main paths. If horseback-riding is new to you, go out to see the horses, observe them, do a course in horseback-riding, feel what meaning horses can have.

Humming Bird

A herald of the rainbow spirit is bringing a new radiance to your everyday life. The iridescent glimmer of a future time of lightness and flexibility, even of exuberance.

Unexpected luck in small things, the promise of a time of inspiration. A buoyant emotional life, the sudden experience of seemingly unfounded blissfulness.

As Card of the Day

Today, unexpectedly, something beautiful will happen, something very cheerful that will live on in your memory.

As Mother Earth

Let your soul swing. Enjoy the little pleasures of life. Whatever might be burdening you now, simply don't take it too seriously!

As Father Sky

Humming birds are rarely seen in Europe. Instead, watch the colorful butterflies fluttering merrily from one blossom to the next, just like the humming birds do. For a few days live like that.

As East

Tomorrow morning get up very early and experience the sunrise at a beautiful place outside in nature.

As South

At noon look for a nice sunny spot, where for a while you can enjoy doing nothing to the fullest.

As West

Step out of your house before sunset and watch the evening sky changing colors on the horizon. Enjoy it silently.

As North

Get up at midnight, sit at the window in the dark and look at the night sky. Feel the peace.

As Medicine

To have this life, to have the opportunity to learn and grow in a human body on this earth and to be able to consciously feel the union with the Great Spirit, is the greatest gift, the greatest bliss there is for us. For four weeks, over and over again intentionally remind yourself of this gift and use this time to make the best of it.

Kachina

A figure personifying certain magical aspects of life on earth or life beyond. Kachinas are often regarded as sacred representatives of the spirits of nature and are worshipped as such. They symbolize special powers that can be activated with their help.

This Kachina is chasing away negative energies with its rattle. Try to feel which negative energies are burdening you. Open up and let your intuition find the right way to dissolve them – with a prayer or a ritual, with incense (a smudge stick) or an intense experience of nature.

As Card of the Day
Look around at your workplace or at home: Which object – maybe a rather ordinary one – carries a secret message for you that you have not noticed up to now?

As Mother Earth
Which women around you do you regard as archetypes of mother and daughter, grandmother and friend? Try to feel what kind of qualities they have for you.

As Father Sky
Which men around you do you perceive as father and son, grand-father and friend? Try to understand why you experience them this way.

As East
Someone has an important message for you.

As South
Someone invites you to enjoy life together.

As West

Someone helps you to overcome the loss of a loved one or to solve a problem.

As North

Someone turns up from whom you can learn much.

As Medicine

Anything can be magic: not only special objects, but even thought and emotional patterns, concepts or traditions. For a month make it your very personal "magic" to be totally honest to yourself. Become aware of the motives that drive you, of the desires that pull you, of the judgments that confine you, of the powers that help you. Be true to yourself!

Kokopelli

The legendary flute player appears in many Red Indian stories and images everywhere between Alaska and Tierra del Fuego. He is a hunchback because he used to travel around as an itinerant trader carrying his goods on his back from one village to the next. He played his flute to call people's attention.

Fertility. A messenger or bearer of gifts is on his way to you. Cheerfully follow your path of the shaman: regardless of the heavy burden of everyday life, your inner music can make your spirit rise.

As Card of the Day

Take some time today to listen to the sound of the flute: Zamfir's panpipes or Mozart's flute concerts… Feel how the flute can lift you up.

As Mother Earth

Is there any living being you could give a present to today? Be like a tree burdened with fruit wanting to feed the hungry.

As Father Sky

Leave the noise of the world behind and listen to the music of life, to the songs of the birds, the gurgling of the brook, the wind in the treetops.

As East

Wander towards the East, to the land promising you a new morning, to the promise of a new path.

As South

Drift to where your heart is pulling you. It is good to be where there is joy and beauty.

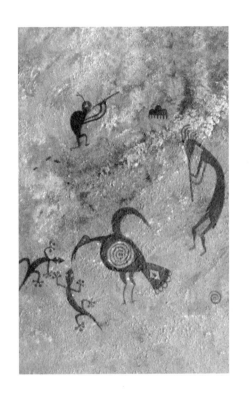

As West

Follow your longing for the light that never dies. You will find it in the music of your soul, inside of you.

As North

Set off to unknown realms, overcoming fears of the unknown. Know that the Great Spirit protects you.

As Medicine

The Kokopelli is a wanderer from one place to the next, a wanderer between worlds and through this strange life. For four weeks live with the awareness that your life, too, is a wandering, leading from here to the horizon, from Mother Earth to Father Sky.

Ladder

A bridge to the invisible worlds. Even if a ladder is not leaning against the wall of a house leading upwards, but is leading us down into the depth of a Kivas, spiritually speaking it always leads us inwards or "upwards".

You are gaining a new access to higher dimensions. Take heart and climb up this ladder. Hold onto it as long as possible and as long as the ladder reaches, then go on climbing up further on the rungs of your spiritual realization.

As Card of the Day

Do you know your goal? If so: What small step towards the great goal can you take today? If not: Start your search today.

As Mother Earth

You will meet a woman who can teach you something about the next steps on your way up.

As Father Sky

You will meet a man who can tell you something about the next steps on your way up.

As East

Sacrifice something on your way up: a prejudice, a thought-pattern, a fixed idea. Let go of it, leave it behind.

As South

Sacrifice something for your advancement: a feeling, a disliking, a preference. Approach someone lovingly.

As West

Sacrifice something for your progress: make an action complete, move house, change your job. Don't bear anyone a grudge for something.

As North

Sacrifice something for your transformation: Try out an unknown method, look for a teacher. Start off on a new path.

As Medicine

What are your "ladders" on the path of the shaman? How do you climb up over the surface of things? Life itself is the ladder, daily meditation and daily selfless service are the rungs that actually allow you to go up. Start climbing!

Medicine Wheel

The four directions East, South, West and North; the four capacities intuition, feeling, instinct and thinking; the four elements fire, water, earth and air (or wind). With this the medicine wheel symbolizes the variety within the unity.

Take your time to find out where you are and what your goals are. Choose the means you need to reach your goals and ask for a higher insight into that which is of best use for all living beings.

Apart from the symbol Zia, the medicine wheel is one of the strongest cards in the Shamanic Oracle.

As Card of the Day

Today a shamanic ritual you are going to carry out will receive special blessings from the Great Spirit.

As Mother Earth

See your whole environment as a big medicine wheel. You are standing in the middle. Look around you: Which feminine power indicates something unusual, maybe even strange? Explore it.

As Father Sky

See your whole environment as a big medicine wheel. You are standing in the middle. Look around you: Which masculine power challenges you to experience something new, maybe even risky? Do it.

As East

Are you pursuing the right goals? Which powers, people and situations are directing you towards them? When and how does your spirit come to rest and experience inner peace?

As South

Do you receive enough strength on your path? Which energies, people and situations give you strength? How does your spirit receive the nourishment it needs?

As West

Are you capable of containing energies that are flowing towards you? Which powers, people and events contain energy? How can you support your ability to remain centered?

As North

From what source do you receive strength? What energies, people and situations give you strength? Find the source from where you can always receive strength.

As Medicine

The Great Spirit calls on you to determine your further spiritual course within the next four weeks and to decide on a path.

Morning Prayer

Start the day with a prayer – with gratitude that you were given the opportunity to live it and with the request to receive help and protection, nourishment and guidance. A symbol of the daily renewed trust in the creative force and the grace of life.

Have trust, be grateful for each day. Continue walking on your path step by step. The most important step is always the one you are taking right now. The most important time is always the moment you are living in right now.

As Card of the Day
Dedicate half an hour in the morning to prayer or meditation. Tune into your determination to be awake, fully aware each minute of the day.

As Mother Earth
To which woman do you owe more than anyone else? For sure your mother. Who else? Show your gratitude, even if this person has died already.

As Father Sky
To which man do you owe more than anyone else? For sure your father. Who else? Teachers, masters? Show your gratitude.

As East
Be grateful to the sun for sending light onto the Earth making us see and experience colors, forms, space.

As South
Be grateful to the sun for warming the Earth – plants, animals and people – making life as such possible at all.

As West

Be grateful to the Earth for letting plants grow that nourish and heal, help us dress and build, thus securing our survival.

As North

Be grateful to the Earth for serving as a support for our feet in the universe and as a soft place for our heads to rest in the night. Without it we would not be able to unfold life.

As Medicine

In the weeks to come be grateful for everything you have got and everything you receive: food and drink, clothes, a roof over your head, your family and friends, your children, your parents, public transport, your work place, medical care, books, conversations, music... Do we have all things necessary? Can we actually take all that for granted?

New Beginning

By working with the medicine wheel a new being arises. The forces of the four directions create something new. Which direction is your foundation, where is your goal?

Sensing possibilities for development; overcoming difficulties; bearing birth pains, striving actively for something completely new; making decisions on which direction to go in the pending transformation.

As Card of the Day

What is it that you have wanted to tackle for a long time, but have postponed over and over again? Start with it today!

As Mother Earth

Serving all living beings selflessly truly is a new beginning. For four weeks live without killing animals (or letting them be killed for you) – in other words: live purely vegetarian.

As Father Sky

The ultimate truths are not visible or tangible, but they can be experienced – like love. Meditating on the "third eye" will lead you toward experiencing ultimate truths.

As East

Start going toward the East – on the inside and on the outside. Revelations are waiting for you there. In Eastern Europe, in India?

As South

Enjoy the South with its warmth, its sweet fragrances, its cheerfulness. Take a break from your everyday life.

As West

Explore the vastness of the West, of the Atlantic coast in the Wild West of America. Make your spirit as vast and open.

As North

Experience the secrets of a midsummer's night, the Northern lights and the nature of Scotland, Sweden or Greenland.

As Medicine

Constant development is a necessity throughout your whole life. Remain open for changes. The learning process never stops. Next month start learning something completely new.

Rain Spirit

Tears rolling down from one eye of the rain spirit are a symbol for the rain, which is synonymous with life-giving grace in primitive tribes. Divine intervention in life or influence from the spiritual world.

Spiritual blessings; also rebirth or spiritual rebirth. You can hope for unexpected blessings, helping you to advance quite a bit further on the path of the shaman. Something is falling "like scales from your eyes. "

As Card of the Day

An incident wants to tell you something; it has a deeper meaning than it seems to have on the surface. Be particularly careful today – an important insight might come to you in the disguise of a seemingly irrelevant event.

As Mother Earth

During the next week experience the weather, every kind of weather, very consciously. Feel the rays of the sun, feel the wetness of the rain, observe the clouds moving across the sky, and open up to a new feeling of oneness with all.

As Father Sky

During the next week go deep into the writings of shamans or saints, seers or Zaddikim, sufis or masters and realize that self-awareness and experiencing the divine are the highest goals in life.

As East

Someone amongst your friends will soon mention a book containing an important new realization for you.

As South

In a couple of days you will experience something in your family which will give you and them a new feeling of solidarity.

As West

In the near future you will meet someone on your path who will show you a new direction.

As North

In the next few days a new opportunity will come up for you to take a jump in your profession.

As Medicine

Learn to cry again – when you are blissfully happy, when you feel compassionate toward other people's misery, when you are grateful for help or longing to become one with the Great Spirit.

Rainclouds

Heavy rainclouds indicating an impending renewal, the revival of old principles and values, as well as the necessary purification of all that has accumulated and unnecessarily hinders any further development.

A new cycle of your personal development is about to begin; your plans and projects will prosper; a time of success in general. A very good sign for the near future.

As Card of the Day

That which could obscure and sadden your mind today will soon turn out to be a great blessing.

As Mother Earth

The earth can only nourish us, if we give something in return and don't only take from it. Look after this creation as much as you can. Care for all living beings and don't destroy life without thinking. Then your whole life will be blessed.

As Father Sky

We can see the sun only if we turn toward it and raise our eyes to the sky. Raise your spirit to the Great Spirit every day, turn to it for prayer or a ritual, for silence or meditation.

As East

Trust in your own strength. You are strong enough to find the answer to your question inside you.

As South

You know already what it is about, and yet you are still afraid to make a decision. Just wait a little more.

As West

It is high time to stop hesitating. Say what needs to be said, do what needs to be done. It is for the best.

As North

Go somewhere to be alone with yourself and ask for more light, more clarity. A dream or vision will show you the right answer.

As Medicine

As a rule, without clouds there is no rain. These precious drops usually don't just fall from the blue sky. Without a master shaman there is no blessing for the path. Go and look for such a meeting, ask for it.

Returning Home

The returning of the spirit; dying, death and that which is happening after life. Shamanic images of beings without arms indicate that they are already on the other side of life.

As long as you have time for it, prepare yourself for the fact that your physical life is limited. Already in this life we have to discover and "practice" our spiritual awareness if we don't want to be lost on the other side.

As Card of the Day

Think of someone you love who has already left this world: What have you learned from him/her? How can you live that yourself today?

As Mother Earth

One day your body will return back to the earth, to the elements of which it is made. Go to a field and take some earth in both of your hands. Feel your original connection with the earth.

As Father Sky

One day your spirit will return back to the Great One across the skies. Let us raise our spirits and become open to sensing and feeling that there is something living in this body which is not from this world.

As East

Start working with the affirmation: "I take in the strength of the color yellow and emanate it."

As South

Start working with the affirmation: "I take in the strength of the color red and emanate it."

As West

Start working with the affirmation: "I take in the strength of the color black and emanate it."

As North

Start working with the affirmation: "I take in the strength of the color white and emanate it."

As Medicine

Our whole life is a returning of the "Prodigal Son" back into the arms of the eagerly waiting, loving father. In order to be able to return back home, we need to know the right direction and to hear the faint call of the Great Spirit. Become receptive to both.

Salamander

In the shamanic tradition, a symbol of transformation similar to that of the alchemists in the Middle Ages for whom the salamander was a symbol of transmutation from lower to higher substances. Like the dragonfly it leads to the water.

You have a special strength or ability inside you that you should take better care of so that you can use its help for the necessary transformation on the path. You will arrive at the "water" of life, once you have changed your shape, shed your old burdens and made your new shape come to life.

As Card of the Day

Which weakness could you transform into a strength today? What can you let go of today, in order to be more open for something more and new?

As Mother Earth

The earth transforms inconspicuous weak seeds into strong and powerful trees. You, too, can transform your plans into reality if you work persistently, use all your strengths wisely and have patience.

As Father Sky

The sky transforms lukewarm air into fierce storms, that which is invisible to the human eye into that which can be wildly felt. You can make your ideals the passion of your life if you allow yourself to be inspired by a higher force.

As East

Go and get a bronze buddha statue, lay some petals around it, light a candle and meditate on its true meaning.

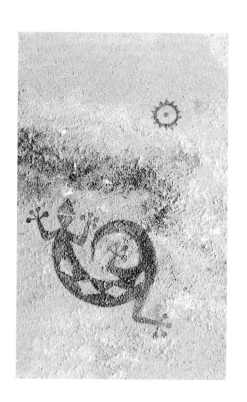

As South

For a few days wear a golden necklace and allow it to remind you of your own innermost nature: of the radiance of the sun waiting for you to live it.

As West

Take a bangle made of copper or a copper nugget and bury it at a place of power you feel particularly drawn to. Open up to love – it will come your way in the next couple of days.

As North

Get yourself a piece of raw iron (from a crystal shop); go to a brook, burn some incense and ask for strength; throw the iron into the water. You will receive strength.

As Medicine

On one day of the week wear a salamander ornament.

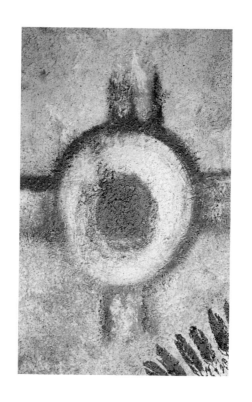

Shield

Protection, tradition, ancient traditional custom, holy rituals, solemn ceremonies; also useful for repulsing attacks of magic powers. The shield is a form of the medicine wheel you can take with you anywhere!

Make use of that which really protects you on your path, which truly benefits you. Allow the wisdom of the elders and their traditional forms to expand your vision and speed up your search.

As Card of the Day

The best protection are serenity and trust in the Great Spirit. Exhale deeply and slowly a few times. Settle within. Surrender your task to a higher force.

As Mother Earth

Go into a cave or a deep, dark gorge. Feel how well protected you are there from the "busyness" of the world. Which elemental forces do you perceive?

As Father Sky

Climb on top of a high mountain, allowing you a panoramic view around. Feel how close you are to the sky and how your spiritual vision of the world is clearing up.

As East

For a few days in a row go to a totem pole (or a tree of power) and stand against it, your face to the East. Close your eyes and feel a subtle strength flowing toward you.

As South

In the next couple of weeks look for objects emanating a special power. Collect them and put them all into a "medicine bundle".

Feel its protection.

As West

Choose a sand image you feel particularly drawn to (if necessary a printed one). Feel its impression on you for a few weeks. What is the secret message it has for your life?

As North

Get yourself a "dream catcher" and put it up in your sleeping room. Over the next few weeks observe if and how your dreams are changing.

As Medicine

Get yourself a shamanic drum, no matter if it is from Africa, Asia or America. Keep drumming – for a long time, and even longer – again and again for a few weeks. Feel how you are gaining strength and confidence.

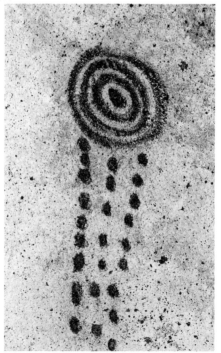

Shooting Star

A message from the ancestors; as a comet also a message from the Great Spirit. Light that flashes up in the sky and dies out shortly afterwards – that is the promise our path of life holds for us through this world: at least shine!

Ask an elderly person two questions today: What has been the most important thing in your life up to now? What kind of advice would you give to someone younger on their path? And: Look for an expert guide.

As Card of the Day

You receive unexpected good news, or you are the one who delivers such news to someone.

As Mother Earth

As suddenly as animals appear in the wilderness and disappear again, opportunities for a breakthrough in life do. Be alert and courageous and seize these opportunities!

As Father Sky

As sudden as a flash of lightning, our life can change in times of upheaval. Be prepared to courageously follow even surprising turns.

As East

You will make a discovery at your workplace which will help you to move on. Use it.

As South

You will come across something at lunch and the truth will begin to dawn on you. Make it yours.

As West

Within your family circle you will come across something or receive something that will bring you more understanding about a certain issue. Apply it.

As North

There is an object in your sleeping room which has got something to do with one of your dreams. Interpret it.

As Medicine

Ask an old person from your vicinity, who does not know you too well, for some advice for your life. Follow this advice for one month to test it.

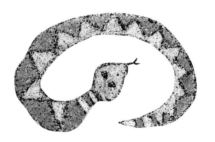

Snake Spirits

These powerful spirits are traveling back and forth between the higher spiritual world and the underworld. They possess a strong medicine: the power of the glimpse into higher and deeper realms of the beyond.

Connection between sky and earth, light and shadow, superconscious and unconscious. Learn to discern where a certain path or certain actions lead you. Look for the light that never dies (see Zia Card).

As Card of the Day

Without silence, contemplation or meditation you will never catch a glimpse of the spiritual realms. Meditate in the twilight hours between day and night.

As Mother Earth

If you haven't the slightest clue how to go on, let go. The earth is nourishing each living being; its spirit gently eases all our difficulties – if we only learn how to let go and trust in its mercy.

As Father Sky

Each single incident in your life has a reason to it. Accept whatever is happening with patience and watch out not to sow the seeds for new harmful causes.

As East

A young woman brings joy into your life.

As South

A strong man helps you to accomplish a task.

As West

An elderly woman shares her wisdom with you.

As North

An elderly man teaches you about unintentional silence.

As Medicine

Don't get deceived by the tempting powers and promises of some spirits. The path of the shaman will lead you to the goal only if you manage to ignore magical powers and spirits from the beyond and if you trust solely in the guidance of the Great Spirit.

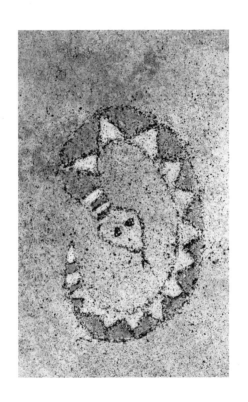

Snake

The proverbial wisdom and healing powers of the snake; a medicine that is difficult to gain, that disappears quickly and is difficult to handle in the right way.

Neither magical powers nor invocations, neither faith nor other miracles are the snake power's goal, but letting go of the ego, self-realization and the understanding that not man but the Great Spirit is the best "medicine man".

As Card of the Day

Do something for your health today: on all levels – physical and spiritual, too. Give yourself the treat of a really invigorating day!

As Mother Earth

Water- or mudbaths in the open, if necessary applying sea salt or mudpacks, will dissolve and wash away toxins that have accumulated in the body and invigorate you.

As Father Sky

Sun- or airbathing at a quiet place, at a lake, in the mountains or on a lonely meadow will very naturally and almost unnoticeably recharge you with a completely new energy.

As East

Rock crystal or diamond will give you support for your spiritual or health problems.

As South

Yellow topaz or rose quartz can help you heal your physical or emotional wounds.

As West

Smoky crystal or aquamarine provide you with the necessary clarity to fulfill your tasks.

As North

Lapis lazuli or garnet give you access to the source of insight into spiritual goals and compassion.

As Medicine

Everything depends on your spiritual health: your physical health, your emotional and mental balance. For the next four weeks stick to a holistic health plan.

Spiral

Symbol of energy; in India also known as the coiled Kundalini-power at the root chakra (which was re-discovered and mis-used in Reiki). An archaic force and at the same time jump starter in order to gain access to other dimensions.

Movement and development are the two main issues of this card. A stop would mean paralysis and death. Therefore it is your responsibility to use and nourish the powers inside and around you that can help you to advance. Learning and struggling, but dancing, too – that's what life is about.

As Card of the Day
Stop going in circles in one particular issue. Climb on top of a tree, instead (in the figurative or literal sense) and gain a new vision.

As Mother Earth
If you really want to understand others, follow their trail of life for one week, step inside their shoes. Then you will develop true understanding.

As Father Sky
No life takes the same course as any other one. Each life is full of it's own demands and challenges. Do not judge others, rather work on yourself.

As East
Look for a new goal if you have reached an old one. Reach out for the stars, for the space behind them.

As South
Whatever you have attained, do not keep it secret but share it with others: goals, powers, skills, knowledge…

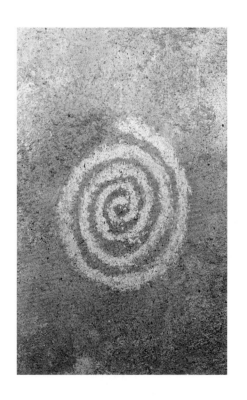

As West

Gain experiences before you set out to help others. Your own development is the prerequisite for being able to effectively help others.

As North

The power to unfold the innermost and the highest comes exactly from there. Go beyond the "I", beyond emotions and mind.

As Medicine

Draw a spiral or get yourself a drawing you like and put it up at home or at your work place. In the next few days keep looking at it consciously, let it be an inspiration for new interpretations and associations; work with its symbolism.

Tortoise

Apart from the coyote and the raven, the image of the tortoise appears in numerous Red Indian myths of creation. It symbolizes protection, willpower, modesty and the capacity to live in two worlds – on land and in the sea.

Trust your instincts, use the resources you already have and find your own pace: "One who walks on his path slowly but steadily, will reach his goal safely."

As Card of the Day

Develop modesty. It is the capacity to cope with each and everything that life brings, no matter if it is a lot or a little, helpful or a hindrance.

As Mother Earth

For some time withdraw into your own four walls; spend your time off with yourself. Find your way back to yourself again.

As Father Sky

For some time go to visit a monastery or a meditation center, go to a mountain hut or into solitude. Stretch out your antennae and tune into the cosmos: What energies are working out there and inside you?

As East

This is a good moment to make a breakthrough and advance safely. Use it!

As South

Make a decision, knowing well that an absolute certainty about right or wrong does not even exist. Follow your heart.

As West

Think before you act. Check where you are before you walk on. Don't rush things.

As North

Ask an old person to discuss a certain issue with you; ask him/her for advice.

As Medicine

Practice patience. Have confidence. Even if all odds seem to be against you, don't freak out. Withdraw into the safety of your soul, go inwards.

Warrior

A shaman with a shield, a "hunter in the skies". The original image of the warrior is not a man who is out to kill others, but rather one who is out to find a higher meaning in life.

Get ready for the most difficult confrontation in your life, trying to find meaning and fulfillment, freedom from emotional patterns and prejudices. Hunting in invisible realms requires the protective shield of courage, decisiveness, persistence and independence from other people's opinions.

As Card of the Day

Throughout the day observe whether you unconsciously simply endorse other people's prejudices or always stay with your own independent opinion.

As Mother Earth

Even our everyday life is a kind of small but progressive "guerilla war" toward the great goal: the realization of spiritual ideals in view of the restrictions imposed on us by the earthly life.

As Father Sky

Follow the highest warpath: the search for meaning. You will have to confront your ego and give up all that is transient, in order to attain to that which is immortal.

As East

Master it that your consciousness will always be full of light, chasing away ignorance like the rising sun dissolving the darkness of the night.

As South

Master it that your feelings will always be full of friendliness towards all living beings like the sun high in the sky sharing its light with all life.

As West

Master it that your actions will be lasting even after some time has passed, like the power of the sun still warming the earth after it has set.

As North

Master it that you will learn the right alone-ness, the all-one-ness, without feeling lonely. Teach all-one-ness to others who feel lonely.

As Medicine

For the next month look at your life as a challenge: a challenge for more clarity and peace, more security and strength, more insight and love.

Water

A river or a stream, a lake or a pond, a waterfall or a brook: all these promise life and fertility. Water is a gift from Mother Earth to keep her children alive, to refresh them and purify them.

Dive into the waves of purification and regeneration, passing the trials on your path without avoiding them. Let other living beings benefit from your skills and gifts.

As Card of the Day

Take a bath of apple cider vinegar and honey, or add sea salt; go to the sauna or to the steam bath; go to swim in a lake or in the sea.

As Mother Earth

No water – no life. Our body consists mainly of water. Plants that consist mainly of water are a good nourishment for the body and hardly put any strain on the mind.

As Father Sky

Water is a part of the great cycle between earth and sky, between the source, the river and the sea and the rain clouds. In times of trial or trouble, remember that they are a blessing, coming "from above".

As East

Morning dew is one of the most precious forms water can take. In the early morning, at sunrise, taste a few drops of this delicious liquid from the flowers.

As South

Use water in the form of hot steam, water contained in plants or essential oils, as a means for inner purification, opening us up.

As West

Dab your temples with the evening dew of grass and leaves. Enjoy the mild coolness and the peace it can bring you.

As North

Water becomes rigid only in the form of ice. When our feelings are frozen, when our gratitude for life has cooled down, we tend to shrink and lose touch with the Great Spirit.

As Medicine

Be liquid, be open; wash out that which is not useful; dissolve that which is too strong; take with you that which is worth taking.

Young Shaman

A shaman's apprentice. Instruction in the art of magic and medicine. A process of spiritually maturing in order to learn how to handle secret knowledge responsibly.

The beginning of a spiritual education; the challenge of combining the spiritual path with everyday life. Trials. The call to discover the inner strength lying behind outer aids such as the rattle or snake medicine; the necessity of purification.

As Card of the Day

Cleanse yourself, have a fasting or fruit day, do some physical exercise that makes you sweat. For a while go out into the open air and breathe deeply; or go into isolation today.

As Mother Earth

For half an hour lie down on the bare ground, on the sand, on a meadow. Start sensing the strength of the earth that carries and nourishes all; sense the blessings of the sky letting the light of life shine on the earth.

As Father Sky

For half an hour stand alternately with your back, then with your belly against a beautiful big tree. Start sensing the strength of the sky letting the tree grow upwards and the strength of the earth giving it strong roots.

As East

Which old childhood dream moves you from time to time? Make it come true now so that you can make the next step.

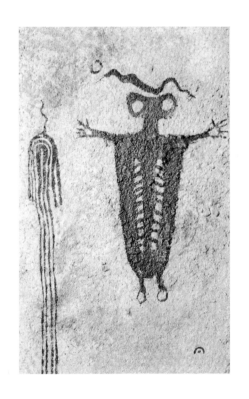

As South

What kind of pleasure would you like to give to someone? Do not spend any more time thinking about it. Just do it!

As West

Which service is someone in your vicinity expecting from you? Don't let him /her wait any longer.

As North

What is it that scares you when you think about old age? Find people who are experiencing this right now and talk to them about it.

As Medicine

Find a master shaman. Don't be content until you find one who will take you to the highest goal, who will not unite you with himself /herself, but with the splendor and the music of the Great Spirit.

Zia

For the shamans of the Southwest, this strange word means "friendship" and "Unity of the Cultures", as well as "Ojo de Dios" – the eye of God. A similar word is known in Islam, meaning "inner light". The symbol of Zia is shown in the center of the New Mexican flag.

Zia is a form of the medicine wheel. Here, too, the point is that you have to decide which path to choose and which means to use. Also, this card reminds you to find the inner light at the "third eye" through meditation and to allow yourself to be taken up to spiritual levels (see The Power of the Soul, Bibliography).

Apart from the medicine wheel, the symbol of Zia is one of the strongest cards in the Shamanic Oracle.

As Card of the Day
Close your eyes and look in front of you at the center of your forehead; gaze into the dark and mentally repeat one of God's names. By and by find the light within.

As Mother Earth
Find a female being and give her the gift of a radiant look in your eyes, a glowing in your heart.

As Father Sky
Find a male being and give him confidence, decisiveness and strength.

136

As East

With the sunrise, a new love is flowering within you. Moving out, a new job, a new beginning in a relationship; in general – new hope.

As South

With the sun at its zenith, love can reach its peak. Projects are turning out well; a piece of work is a success; a relationship is fulfilling; in general – a fresh impetus.

As West

With the evening sun, the love that already exists is deepening. Projects come to an end; a piece of work is completed; a relationship matures; in general – a time of harvest.

As North

With the night, love is tried and tested for quite a while; projects are doubted; a piece of work comes to a halt; a relationship has to overcome conflicts; in general – a time of trial.

As Medicine

Look for silence in the midst of the noise of the world. In the course of the next month find the time to meditate silently every day. Focus your attention on the innermost being.

I Am an Eagle

Questions and Interpretation
of the Shamanic Oracle:

I am an eagle.
The small world laughs at my acts.
But the Great Sky keeps my thoughts
of immortality to itself.

Song from the Taos Pueblo

It is up to us how we use the Shamanic Oracle. What feelings and thoughts do we cherish while asking for advice? Let the petty world smile at us as we are consulting these images! While we are soaring like eagles in the other, spiritual dimensions, we will gain insights and derive benefits that will remain invisible to the eyes of people who are interested only in the material world and intellectual logic. These images reach the soul directly.

In practice, you can use these cards similarly to the way you use tarot cards. In any case, you should take enough time for questioning and interpreting the cards. The questioners may perform their own individual little ceremony or develop their own ritual.
It is recommended to take a few deep breaths of fresh air (if necessary at the window or on the balcony) while preparing for the question internally.

It is best to pose only one question at a time. The more precisely you formulate it, the clearer will be the answer that you'll receive.

You can use a blanket, a cloth or a fur for spreading out the cards. You might want to burn wild sage or a smudge stick. Or you may decide to consult the cards outdoors, in nature, in the open air.

What kind of questions can you ask or are you supposed to ask? Any one that is really important to you. You can focus on small or big issues. Accordingly, there are different ways of interpreting. However, the most expressive answers the Shamanic Oracle gives are in response to questions that have to do with our direction in life, higher goals, facing big challenges or the search for meaning. Maybe writing down the question will help you to focus better!

When you are ready, sit down and shuffle the cards carefully – there is no reason to hurry – and think of your question.

Once you feel inside that now is the right moment for spreading the cards, lay them out in front of you. You can fan them in a circle like in the medicine wheel or in any other form you choose.

Then start selecting the cards one by one according to their positions in the spread of your choice. Lay them out facing down.

Gather the rest of the cards and get ready for the Great Spirit talking to you through the Shamanic Oracle. Slowly turn over the chosen cards one by one. Now, meet yourself!

One Card of the Day – One Card

Select one card for the day. What energy, what symbol, what animal, what image is important for you today? This interpretation is valid only for this particular day.

Model Questions

1. What is demanding my special attention today?
2. Which gift can I use sensibly today?
3. What lesson is there for me to learn today?

Mother Earth / Father Sky – 2 Cards

Select two cards: The first one represents Mother Earth, the second one Father Sky. Mother Earth is showing us our worldly tasks, Father Sky our spiritual goals. Additionally, both cards symbolize yin and yang, feminine and masculine energies, anima and animus, the visible creation (Mother Earth) and the invisible spirit of creation (Father Sky), as well as the many polarities or dualities we experience in everyday life. This interpretation is valid for two days or two weeks, but no longer than two months.

Model Questions

1. What issue do I have to accomplish or solve now?
2. Which goal should I aim at in the near future?

1. Which feminine aspect should I give more space?
2. Which male energy should I develop further?

1. What gift does Mother Earth want to give to me?
2. What insight does Father Sky want to impart to me?

This type of interpretation is particularly suitable for relationship questions, as it clearly expresses the different opinions, attitudes and behavior patterns of two persons. With these cards it is obvious that usually they do not point out opposites, but simply a different focus (the only exceptions are: the "Water"- and the "Fire" Cards).

Model Questions for Relationship Issues

1. What is important for the woman in this relationship?
2. What is important for the man in this relationship?

1. What part plays the woman in this relationship?
2. What part plays the man in this relationship?

1. What does the woman expect from the man?
2. What does the man expect from the woman?

The Course of Time – 3 Cards

Select three cards. The first one symbolizes the past, the second one the present and the third one the future. "The Past" stands for a period of time a few days or weeks ago, but no longer than one to three months ago. "The Present" means today or one of these days or this week, and "The Future" indicates a period within the next few days or weeks, but no later than the next one to three months.

Model Questions

1. Which unfinished task from the past is still important for me today?
2. What new task do I have to accomplish at present?
3. What new task in the near future is waiting for me to tune into now?

1. What kind of messages do I receive from my deceased ancestors from the spiritual world?
2. What kind of messages do I receive from the Earth right now?
3. What kinds of messages from the Great Spirit are awaiting me in the near future?

1. Which old path do I have to follow one more time?
2. What is the best way for me to follow my present path?
3. Where do I find a new path?

The Medicine Wheel – 4 Cards

Select four cards. The first one indicates the East, the second one the South, the third one the West and the fourth one the North. This spread points out places of power and/or appropriate powers waiting to be brought out now in certain behavior patterns in the questioner's life. The spread is valid for four weeks or four months.

The Meaning of the Card Positions

1. East: fire, spirit, intuition –
           sun, yellow, goal oriented
2. South: water, emotions, feelings –
           plants, red, empowering
3. West: earth (as an element), experience, instinct –
           Earth (as planet), black, containing strength
4. North: wind (air), mind, thinking –
           animals, white, receiving strength

(Where would you find man? A conscious man is at home in the middle of the medicine wheel, an unconscious one would probably feel most comfortable in the animal kingdom.)

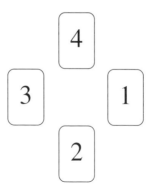

Model Questions

1. What kind of medicine can help the spirit to take wing?
   This card refers to the power of significant goals.
2. What kind of medicine can dissolve emotional blocks?
   This card refers to the power of constructive feelings.
3. What kind of medicine can be a support for my actions?
   This card refers to the power of helpful experiences.
4. What kind of medicine can help me think clearer?
   This card refers to the power of holistic reason.

1. How can I strengthen my intuition?
2. How can I deepen my feelings?
3. How can I become less selfish in my actions?
4. How can I become more rooted to the earth in my thoughts?

You can also use the medicine wheel in a simply geographical sense: Find out what activities or experiences could be associated with the four directions, using your apartment or house, your home country or place of birth as reference points.

1. What promises does the East make?
2. What does the South want?
3. What does the West demand?
4. What does the North think?

Vision Quest – 7 Cards

A vision quest is a spiritual search that is pursued with full intention and yet with no guarantees, with full attention and yet without any particular expectation. Success is a gift given by the Great Spirit; success cannot be "made".

This spread connects the theme of Mother Earth/Father Sky with the theme of the medicine wheel, referring to a particular image, a very special place of power and a very personal medicine. The first two cards are selected for Mother Earth and Father Sky – they are placed in the middle. The next four cards are placed at the four positions of the medicine wheel, starting from the East, via the South and the West, to the North. The last card symbolizes the personal medicine. This spread is valid for seven weeks or seven months.

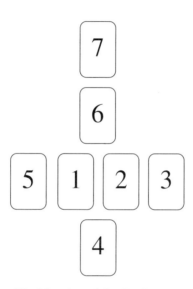

The Meaning of the Card Positions

1. Mother Earth
2. Father Sky
3. East
4. South
5. West
6. North
7. Medicine; also: the very core of the question and the "Key Card"

1. What can I learn from Mother Earth?
   What am I supposed to give to Mother Earth?
2. What can I learn from Father Sky?
   What am I supposed to give to Father Sky?
3. How can I find a spiritual goal that helps me to advance?
   spring, sprouting, new beginning, life, awakening
4. What joy for others can flower through me?
   summer, flowering, abundance, sensuality, stability
5. What work can I do for others?
   autumn, harvest, balance, comfort, fulfillment
6. How do I learn to let go of the inessential?
   winter, passing, farewell, death, change
7. What medicine does the Great Spirit send to me?

Open Spread

Traditionally, oracles are consulted with the cards concealed: meaning that the cards face downward when you spread or select them. This is to fully bring out the power of the unconscious which – by interacting with the law of synchronicity – makes us select the card or the cards most adequate to the question.

However, with certain questions, asking for ways of becoming conscious, or in particular therapeutic situations it has proved useful to spread the cards facing upward before selecting one. Why? Because this way the attention of our eyes is caught by images we feel particularly drawn to and our waking consciousness is activated even more.

In some situations an open rather than a concealed spread is more beneficial to some people, especially if the questioner considers consulting the cards to be "psychic mumbo-jumbo" or "esoteric occult superstition."

When using the open spread, after having thoroughly studied all the images, you can consciously select three cards each for the following positions:

1. This card describes my present situation the best.
2. This card represents the biggest problem I am facing right now.
3. This card refers to the best way to help with the problem or to solve it.

Or:

1. I feel drawn most to this card.
2. This card repulses me the most.
3. This card makes me feel balanced.

Then, start reading the explanations in the book and ask yourself, or discuss with your consultants or therapists, why you selected one card or another, how you could make even better use of your own powers and dissolve sources of disturbance or blocks. (For sessions and seminars with the author see reference to address in the appendix.)

The Great Winds

Sometimes I am absorbed in self-pity.
And yet the Great Winds
keep carrying me across the sky.

Song of the Ojibwa

On our journey across Mother Earth we humans drown in self-pity or dullness from time to time – in the "developed" countries even more so than in the so-called Third World. How many people around us are affected by this? Does it affect us, too, again and again?

Just have a look around you: How many faces radiate the bright light of the sun in the day? How many faces have the soft glow of the moon at night? Through how many eyes does the Great Spirit shine through? And how many people see the Great Spirit in all living beings?

How many people have the strength of the bear, the wisdom of the raven, the message of the buffalo, the grace of the deer, the dexterity of the coyote, the courage of the wolf, the abundance of the prairie, the silence of the woods, the depths of the earth, the heights of the sky?

How many people cherish the memory of their ancestors, live in active compassion toward living beings and in awe of the Great Spirit? Have we forgotten nearly everything? Have we lost our heritage?

Even if we drown in self-pity from time to time, the Great Winds still keep carrying us further on our way through this life… Just remember: We have all existed long before Mother Earth gave us this little body and fed it at its bosom until it grew bigger. And we will continue to exist long after we have returned this same body that meanwhile became old, long after we have gone over to the spiritual world. The Great Spirit knew us when we were still with Father Sky and it is waiting for us to come back to it at the end of our journey.

How can we get rid of self-pity? How can we enter the heritage of our ancestors and preserve it? How can we realize what our mission is and fulfill it? How can we walk the path of the shaman and bring it to life?

By taking responsibility! By understanding deeply from our head, heart and belly, from our intuition, mind and instinct, by thinking, feeling and sensing, that there is only one single person who can guide us through life: we, ourselves!

At its deepest core, the path of the shaman means to trust in the Great Spirit that its winds will carry us further as soon as we make up our minds to walk the path, no matter how hesitant our first own steps might be, how imperfect we might be, how many times we might stumble, fall over or, temporarily, even collapse.

No one but you is capable of knowing your tasks; no one but you is capable of following your own path. No one but you can let the sun shine from your heart again. No one but you can honor and care for the earth that carries and nourishes you. No one but you can raise your eyes to the blue sky and let yourself be carried from the visible to the invisible world.

No one but you can listen to the first timid sounds of the fresh green buds sprouting up in spring; no one but you can join in the cheerful song of summer that is carried over the vast lands; no one but you can rejoice in the music of autumn, celebrating harvest; and, finally, no one but you can hear the sweet tune beckoning you to follow the light beyond darkness in winter.

Find your Mother Earth, your Father Sky, find your Pole Star – find the Great Spirit in yourself!

"All things began with a vision. All things have their origin in the vision. Yet, all things still need to be put into action.

All that is, that comes into being, that is produced or created, is a result of a doing or carrying out. Even the vision itself has a cause to it:

We have to search for it. We have to look for visions and dreams, and then live our dreams."

(From: *Welt des Wissens: Der Gesang des Donnervogels,* The World of Knowledge: The Song of the Thunderbird, pg. 40, published by O.W. Barth Verlag, Bern/München)

Bibliography

- Benedikt, Johann (publisher): *Erinnert euch an eure Menschlichkeit (Remember that You Are Human)*, published by Urania Verlag, CH-Neuhausen (Switzerland) 1998;

- Büsing, Antje (publisher): *Auf den Spuren der Weisheit – Gedanken für jeden Tag des Jahres aus den Religionen der Welt (Following the Tracks of Wisdom – Thoughts for Every Day of the Year From the Religions of the World)*, published by Gütersloher Verlagshaus, Gütersloh 1997.

- Singh, Darshan: *Spiritual Awakening*, published by S.K. Publications, 1982;

- Singh, Rajinder: *Power of the Soul – Instructions for spiritual development*, German version published by Urania Verlag, CH-Neuhausen (Switzerland) 1997;

- Singh, Rajinder: *Empowering Your Soul through Meditation*, Element Books 1999;

- von Rohr, Wulfing: *Licht in der Stille – Ein Stundenbuch über Sterben und Leben (Light in the Silence – An Hour-to-Hour Book on Living and Dying)*, published by Urania Verlag, CH-Neuhausen (Switzerland) 1998;

- von Rohr, Wulfing: *Der Seelenquotient – Was ist Ihr SQ? Wie Sie Ihr ganzes Potential entfalten (The Soul Quotient – What is Your SQ? How to Develop Your Potential Fully)*, published by Goldmann Verlag, München 1988;

- von Rohr, Wulfing: *Das Buch der Meister – Wer sie sind und warum wir sie brauchen (The Book of the Masters – Who They Are and Why We Need Them)*, published by Knaur Verlag, München 1998;

- Winter, Gayan S., von Rohr, Wulfing: *Tarot der Liebe (Tarot of Love)*, card illustrations by Marcia Perrry; cards published by

AGMüller, CH-Neuhausen (Switzerland); book published by Ariston Verlag, Kreuzlingen 1994; www.tarotworld.com

– Winter, Gayan S., von Rohr, Wulfing: *Kraft der Engel – Wegweiser durchs Jahr (The Power of Angels – A Guide Throughout the Year)*, card illustrations by Gayan S. Winter, text by Wulfing von Rohr, published by Urania Verlag, CH-Neuhausen (Switzerland) 1996;

About the Artist

Kenneth Joseph Estrada was born in Santa Fe as a descendant of an old Spanish family who settled in the American Southwest many centuries ago. He was initiated into the Path of the Red Indian Shamans by elders who chose not to be mentioned here by name. Ken is a sensitive artist, who is inspired by the wisdom of the Anasazi Shamans. Their wisdom is reflected in the nearly disintegrated rock drawings you can find almost everywhere in the Land of Enchantment. He creates signs and images that bring back to life the Great Spirit of the Elders, but in a way that makes the archetypes and symbols accessible to the modern man. If you are interested in his work (he offers the pictures on these cards as original paintings), you can contact him directly at: 1920 Thomas Avenue, Santa Fe, NM 87505.

About the Author

Wulfing von Rohr is a TV journalist and yoga teacher, a leader of seminars and a meditator. He is the author and co-author of more than fifty books on self-realization, natural health and spiritual paths. He is a leading expert in the fields of spirituality, meditation and mysticism in Europe. During his twelve-year stay in Santa Fe he filmed a TV documentary for the ZDF (a major German TV channel) on the extinct civilization of the Anasazi in the Chaco Canyon, which was broadcast in the USA as well; along with it he published a TV tie-in. At present, he lives in Europe. For consultation, lectures or seminars you can contact him at the following address: Wulfing von Rohr, Angererstr. 12, D-83346 Bergen; phone: 0049-8662-5842, fax: 419553; e-mail: wulfing@12move.de.